SEESAW
BOOKS™

MY FAVORITE
FRIENDS

Written by Rosie Reed

Illustrated by Mari Goering

MODERN PUBLISHING
A Division of Unisystems, Inc.
New York, New York 10022

The mail carrier visits our house almost every day, bringing letters and cards from far away. Mail carriers deliver magazines and packages, too. Our mail carrier picks up the letters that I want to send to my grandparents. He is busy all day long, picking up and delivering the mail all over town.

Published by Modern Publishing
A Division of Unisystems, Inc.

Copyright ©1989 by Modern Publishing,
A Division of Unisystems, Inc.

TM–SEESAW BOOKS is a trademark owned by Modern Publishing,
a Division of Unisystems, Inc.

®—Honey Bear Books is a trademark owned by Honey Bear
Productions, Inc., and is registered in the U.S. Patent and
Trademark Office.

Printed in Singapore

The mail carrier is bringing letters.

When I go to school or out to play, a friendly policeman watches out for me. He helps me cross busy streets. The police make sure that our town is peaceful and safe. I can trust the police to help me if I'm in trouble or far from home and lost.

The policeman helps me cross streets.

I like to go shopping with Mommy at the grocery store. Our grocer sells fruits and vegetables. She sells many other things, too, like soap and toothpaste. The grocer is very nice and she always remembers how much I like oranges.

The grocer sells oranges.

My stuffed animals are special friends. I like to pretend that they can talk and walk, and sometimes I dress them up in funny clothes. I like to tell them secrets, and I like to sing to them, too. Sometimes Mommy washes them, and I miss them while they have their bath. But soon they're clean and soft, and ready to play with me again.

My stuffed animals are soft.

Firefighters are important friends. They help people. They help animals, too. When my little kitten was afraid to come down from a high tree branch, the fireman helped get her out of the tree, safely. If there's ever a fire, the firefighters rush to put it out. They don't want anyone to get hurt. Firefighters are brave and strong.

Firefighters help people.

My doctor is caring and helpful. She takes care of sick people and she helps me to stay healthy. When I visit her office, the doctor checks my ears, eyes, nose, and throat. She makes sure my body is working just the way it is supposed to. When I grow up, maybe I'll be a doctor and take care of people, too.

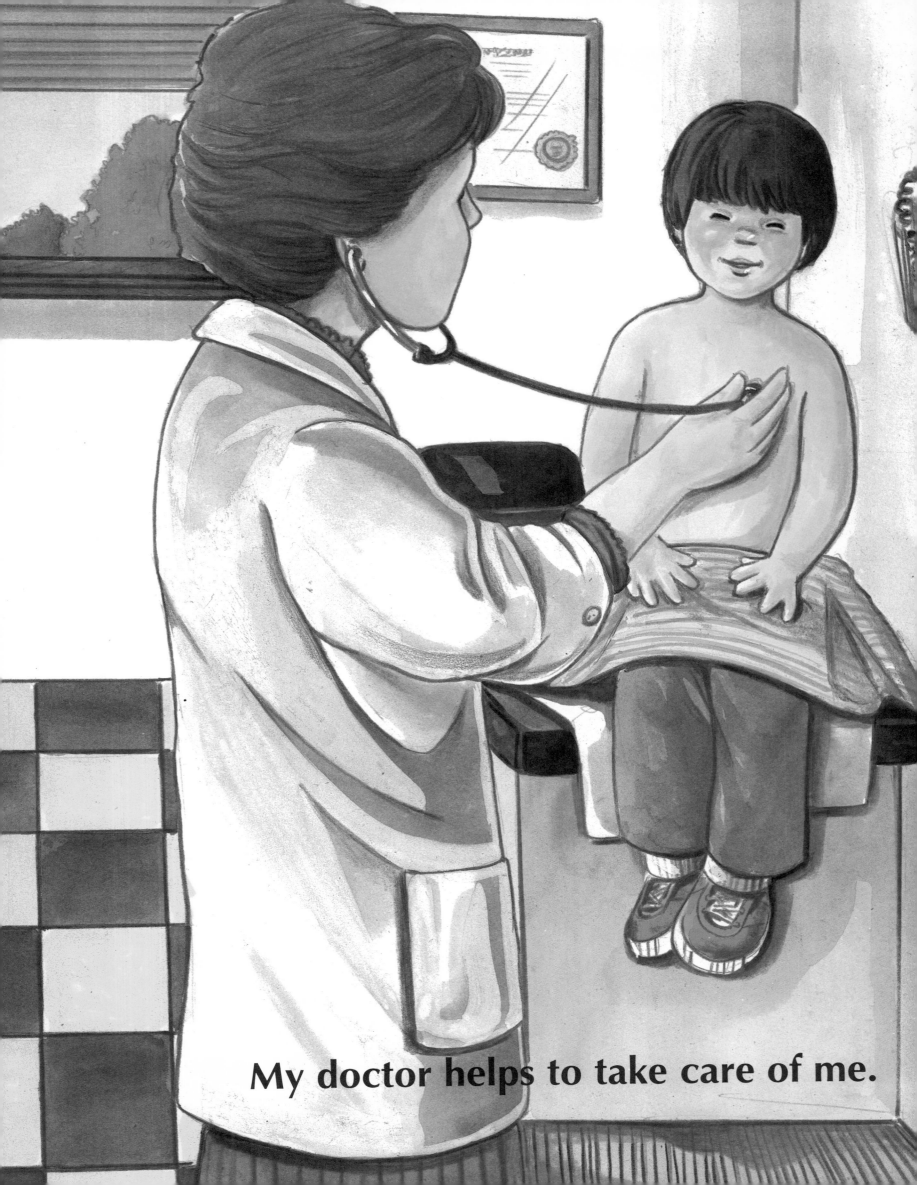

My doctor helps to take care of me.

I love my puppy. He and I have lots of fun playing together. We chase butterflies or go exploring in the backyard. Sometimes we are quiet together, and, every night, my puppy sleeps in my room with me. My puppy and I are good friends.

I have fun with my puppy.

The very best friends I have are my parents. Mommy and Daddy each take good care of me. They show me what food is good to eat and what clothes are right to wear. They show me how to be fair and kind to others. They help me to have fun and stay safe. I love my parents and they love me.

Mommy and Daddy are good to me.